From A Mess To A Miracle To A *Messenger*

Cyteria Freeman

From A Mess To A Miracle To A Messenger
Cyteria Freeman

Published by Pecan Tree Publishing,
July 2010
Hollywood, Fl.
www.pecantreebooks.com

This book or parts thereof may not be reproduced in any form, stored in a retrieval system, or transmitted in any form by any means – electronic, mechanical, photocopy, recording, or otherwise – without prior written permission of the publisher, author or legal representative of both parties, except as provided by United States of America copyright law.

Article printed on page 11 reprinted with permission of the Daytona Beach News-Journal.

Copyright 2010 by Cyteria Freeman

Library of Congress Control Number: 2010932084

ISBN: 978-0-9821114-5-1

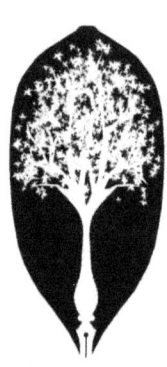

PECAN TREE PUBLISHING

www.pecantreebooks.com

New Voices | New Styles | New Vision

I dedicate my life and this book to my Lord and Savior
Jesus Christ;
without Him, I am certain I would not be here to share my story with you.

I dedicate this book to
my father – **Willie Frank Williams**
and
my mother – **Lizzie Lue Williams**

Who can find a virtuous woman for her worth is far above rubies.
Her children rise up and call her blessed.
Charm is deceitful and beauty is passing, but a woman who fears the Lord, she shall be praised.

Proverbs 31: 10, 28 and 30

My deepest and sincere appreciation and love to my husband, **John Freeman**; your support and encouragement throughout this project were invaluable. I love you dearly.

To my sister **Patricia Williams**, you played a big part in this project, you helped write, read, listen and gave creatively. We laughed and cried together as we wrote remembering the past. I could not have done it without you.

To all of my other **brothers and sisters as well as my half-sister and my nieces and nephews** – know that I love you dearly.

To my five children – **Treniqua, Shawntrell, Brian, Michael and Markquis** – thank you for being a blessing in my life; and for loving me after all we have been through. The best is still yet to come.

To my grandchildren **Jasmine, Precious, Daric, Zaria, and Savannah** – words cannot express the joy you have brought to my life.

To **Aunty Rose** for your support and encouragement and for always reminding that I can according to: Philippians 4:13: "I can do all things through Christ which strengthens me."

To the staff at **Rising Star Day Care** and **Preschool** – thank you for encouraging me to keep pressing toward my vision.

To my pastors, **Pastor Tony Barhoo** and **Co-Pastor Sharlene Barhoo**, I appreciate you for recognizing the miracle working power of God in my life.

To **Pastor Jeffrey Robinson** and **First Lady Valencia Robinson** for training and preparing me for the next level in ministry – thank you.

Dr. Patti Hall-Pennell, thank you for using your expertise to bring out the best in me at Daytona State College.

Hellen L. Green, **Edweater L. Page** and family - your financial support and encouragement is applauded.

To **Charles** and **Juaneishia Smarr**, may God bless you richly for the seed of faith you have sown into my ministry.

To **Charles Smarr**, thank you so much for your creative and technical support of my ministerial efforts. May God enlarge your territory and open doors for you.

To my writing coach, **E. Claudette Freeman** and **staff** for going beyond the call of duty with this book and making one of my dreams come true.

The Message That Comes From Allowing a Miracle Out of Your Mess

God in all His marvelous power created mankind and gave him the breath of life. Man was created with purpose, plan and destiny. Everything man needed for survival was given at creation. Life was supposed to be adventurous and exciting; however, it is full of challenges and chores. The cosmic battle between the righteous forces of God, and the demonic forces of evil, continue to play out in thousands of ways. The battle between good and evil creates a constant wave of spiritual warfare.

Our enemy seeks to conquer and destroy the spirit, body and soul. Even though the enemy is invisible to the naked eye, his opposition is real. The battle for our destiny began at birth. Demons were unleashed from the pits of hell with an assignment to destroy us. However, God has a covering over our lives. The same test given to Job is now given to us. Will you quit, give up, go back or let go? Your answer must be, "Absolutely not!" If God is for you, who can be against you?

I believe just as God spoke of Job, He spoke of this woman of God, "Have you considered my servant, Cyteria?"

Minister Cyteria Freeman was destined to win. Her passion and determination gave her the power to run this race. She realized the road to victory is not always easy, but it is not impossible. The choices she made determined her outcome.

Her life is the perfect example that brings hope to those that do not see a way out. She knew that God did not design her to fail, to be defeated, or to be overcome by life's situations. God gave her the power to be victorious.

The personal testament of Minister Freeman will encourage, motivate and bless you. She shows that all things are possible if you believe. Her faith in God made all the difference. Although, she faced addiction issues, family failures, financial turmoil, relationship problems, mental and emotional traumas, she held on to the promises of God. She had the right attitude. Minister Freeman realized she was not made for the problem, but the problem was made for her. How long she stayed in the problem was determined by her attitude. She saw her obstacles as opportunities and her setbacks as a way to come back.

I want to personally recommend this book to anyone who feels like giving up; to those engaged in spiritual battle or dealing with some form of addiction; to those who are overwhelmed by life's expectations and to those born with a divine destiny. Know that God loves you, and has promised never to leave nor forsake you. You can do all things through Christ Jesus that strengthens you. The Bible declares, "No weapon that is formed against thee shall prosper…" (Isaiah 54:17). God has given you the power to pull down every stronghold in your life.

My prayer is that the test and testimonies in this book would break yolks off of your life, and allow you to enjoy the favor of God.

Apostle Tony Barhoo,
Founding and Senior Pastor
Living Faith World Ministries
Daytona Beach, Fl

THE BLOOD OVERCOMES

"And they overcame him by the blood of the lamb and by the word of their testimony..."
Revelation 12:11a

If you ever thought that you could not be used by God because of your past, think again! This book provides indisputable proof that your past can be used by God as a spring board to your promise. Yes! God can transform your mess into a miracle. Furthermore, this book demonstrates that transparent testimonies have the power to transform lives.

Moreover, it is hard to contain my excitement over this publication. I have been blessed to witness the tremendous growth of a wife, mother, student, preacher and now author. Cyteria Freeman is a woman of great devotion, diligence, and determination. I am privileged to have such a gifted daughter in the ministry.

I am confident that wherever you are in your walk with Christ, this book will inspire and encourage you to know that all things are working together for your good. If you are unsaved, I pray that this book will help you to see and receive the transforming power of God's unconditional love.

Pastor Jeffrey Robinson, Senior Pastor
Mount Carmel Missionary Baptist Church
Daytona Beach, Fl

CHAPTER 1

The Monster Was Raging Again

"Pumpkin! Pumpkin! Stop it now! Come on over here! Enough is enough now. Act right and come here."

The monster was raging again. I was on another seething trip driven by my high. Fighting was not an unusual thing for me. I was a fighter. All you had to do was look at me wrong, or for that matter all I had to do was think you looked at me wrong and I was ready to fight. The fighting would intensify if you actually spoke to me in a manner that I considered harsh. Hello, honestly, could have sounded harsh to me depending on the level of my feel good at that particular moment.

"Pumpkin get in the car! Get in the car now!"

The voice of my brother-in-law's nephew still bangs in my ears so clearly. He would pick me up off the streets so many times for fighting. His voice would be so loud and stern from his patrol car loud speaker.

"Pumpkin, Pumpkin you gonna get arrested for disorderly conduct. Come here; come get in the car right now!"

I would stumble to the car still talking trash, still ready to fight and yet respecting his authority and the fact that he would not take me to jail. Instead he would take me to family – my sister or my mom. I am sure he wished they would find a way to keep me out of the streets before another police officer grew tired of my foolishness. I mean everybody knew Pumpkin and everybody knew I would fight – with or without reason. I remember several times when a former lover would come looking for me after I would be gone from home and my children for days on end. His discovery of me would always lead to arguments; arguments would always lead to fist fights.

I imagine we would have been one of the featured fights passed around on email if that type of thing was popular then.

Then, was the late 70's/early 80's. I was living the high life. My high life did not entail big fancy cars, extravagant housing full of the latest from the interior design industry. My high life was just that – days of getting high, higher and higher still. My high life was an excruciating descent into hell at the invitation of the demon that kept seducing every thing I was convinced I needed.

MATTHEW 8:16

When the even was come, they brought unto him many that were possessed with devils: and he cast out the spirits with his word, and healed all that were sick:

CHAPTER 2

A Young Thing With A Nice Smile

In the tenderness of my 15th year of life, I gave birth to my first child and stepped into the spiraling effects of so much emotional upheaval. Growing up in the South Side projects of Daytona Beach, Florida, I had come familiar with rejection. My Daytona was not the one marketed on tourism brochures attracting the large motorcycle gangs that would gather. It was not the beach beautiful city where throngs of high school and college students would flock looking for a party and sensual romance with no questions asked. It was the projects, where the money was low, the crime was high and whatever you needed to drown your sorrows was readily available.

My first baby daddy loved me enough to get my most precious gift, and then he dumped me and disrespected me like I was nothing more than a two dollar one night stand he had paid for. The rejection hit me hard; so hard in fact that I dropped out of Spruce Creek High School; the place where I should have learned so much more about history and algebra. Instead I experienced the painful lessons of a broken heart and took a class in the wrong things to heal the pain. I just could not take the nasty remarks and the even more vicious looks. A friend introduced me to this club, where no one cared what kind of baggage you came in with me, I was a young thing with a nice smile and the men gave me all kinds of wonderful attention. I loved that attention. The club became my classroom and I became one of its best students.

I began to go through all kind of experiences and dealt with all kinds of people. No one was a stranger to me. I considered everybody a friend even those that chose to live a homosexual life style. I always had love and compassion for people; so much so that on occasion I would allow different females to live with me. One of those acts of compassion introduced me to yet another heart break experience, when I discovered she felt so comfortable in my home that she became comfortable in my relationship as well. My heart shattered into a thousand pieces when I found out that she was sleeping with my man. After that there was no reason to continue in either relationship, I began to go on this rollercoaster ride in and out of relationships with no sense of direction I began having baby after baby from different men. This was the beginning of a degree I earned from being in the streets. In the streets, you learn things that no text book can teach you. The name of the game is survival and only the strong survive.

I probably could not give you the exact date. I know that I cannot tell you it was a sunny day or rainy day. I was weary of men that were not the lovers of my soul. They were men who were merely concerned with what intimate favors they could convince me to provide. There was no love in the arms of these boys or men as it were. Honestly, even if it was, it was not the depth or definition of love that I longed for or needed.

The love that I desired was the kind that a daughter shared with her father. It was the emotion that came with images you would see on television. The images of fathers pushing their daughters on neighborhood swings; or romping with them in tall, beautiful green grass – those were not the colors painted on the canvas of my life. My father was one of Daytona's most notorious drug dealers. My father was, without intending any disrespect and simply stating a fact, very whorish. His attachment to my mom meant she endured a lot of heartache, tears and frantic roller coaster rides of emotions. Yet she did it with a certain dignity. She was not the kind of woman who would run behind him and beg his return. Instead she focused on raising her children and assuring their bellies were full.

My rejection was born with my father. While I hold no animosity or ill-feelings toward him, I also knew that while he acknowledged me and respected my position as his daughter; there was never any deep emotional attachment. The relationship that many psychologists believe dictates how a woman interacts with a man that of a woman and her father was one of distance and rejection. Rejection therefore became the theme in my romantic relationships. Their characters much like my father, detached and whorish at best. Still, I would fall for the sweet words and soft squeezes offered in apologies and consistently end up in relationships with lovers who without fail would reject me and leave me. Despite the disrespect and distance where love was supposed to be blooming and thriving; I would stay in place faithfully and dutifully loving the unfaithful bad boy. I did what I saw my mother do with my dad, until she just stopped doing it.

CHAPTER 3

The Place to Help You Feel Good

It, was around the time that the 70s sashayed off the scene and allowed the 80s to take their place, that the projects and the streets of Daytona Beach were abuzz with this new thing. The projects where I lived surely resemble those in other urban neighborhoods across America. The neighborhood was full of rows of housing units that were almost carbon copies of each other. The neighborhood burst at the seams with poor and lower income middle in the actual project units; and middle class families in the small but nicer houses that were built on the perimeter of the projects. Those homes were primarily older people raising families who had settled in many years earlier lived.

The Southside projects were a traditional Black neighborhood where if you needed to borrow a cup of sugar or ketchup you could always get it. My mother never liked for us to borrow things; but it was what you did to survive some days. From our section of the project, Turie T. Small Elementary School sat right across the street. Needless to say it was the school that throngs of us would rush to each morning and run home from every afternoon. That is of course unless someone was engaged in one of those famous "I'm gone get you after school" battles.

Just like other project communities there was the corner store that most people hung out at. There also was no lack of liquor stores (or package stores as they were called), little night clubs and of course places of worship. Our corner store was on the other side of a path that ran through a section of the housing units – Pearson's. Many of us called it Bo's, because that was the name of that man that ran it. We would spend hours playing in our project world; the boys on the basketball court and the girls watching the boys on the basketball court. There was also a park where the younger kids hung out and their older sisters and brothers pretended to watch them.

We, of course, had neighborhood bullies. We would fight every day and then be best friends by the time we headed across the street or down the road to the schools that served us from kindergarten through graduation. We had our issues, there were knife fights, there were times when whole families would be fighting against each other and people would actually be shooting from one apartment into another. We were central Florida's version of the wild Wild West.

My first apartment in the projects was Apt. 89. It had two bedrooms and it was upstairs facing the woods. Then I moved into another place Apt. 92 and my last project apartment was Number 58. Why the apartment numbers remain so clear to me; while other details of my dark period do not – I really cannot say. Some of the buildings were like a cream/tan color and others were rusting from water wear. Growing up, we had a three bedroom unit, and the windows had some type of metal sheeting along the bottom of them – the project version of iron bars as a security measure. We had a fruit tree in the front yard; others planted flowers and trees to give their subsidized housing the flair of a community on the rise.

The projects were already the place to help your feel-good feel even better, but I do not believe even Southside was ready for what this new little rock formed drug was about to bring. This new thing promised an escape from every thing that life was handing you that you did not want to deal with. The formal invitation to the central Florida community came at the hands of a drug boy out of Miami. He said it was going to make money and it was going to make everyone who kissed it feel real lovely.

I could have taken him at his word but that was not good enough. He made this hot commodity sound better than any product promoted by a well-paid advertising agent. I liked his advertisement and bought into what he was selling - literally. As the drug started flowing from corner to corner, my sister and I were in the thick of it. She was younger than me and had already dibbled and dabbled in different narcotics. She and I were always partners in crime, always into something like sneaking out the bedroom window to the dances in Campbell School's gym. Sure my mom had laid the hammer down and said we could not go for one reason or another; but surely she didn't want us to not show off our moves beneath the disco lights. The gym was transformed and it would be like the teenagers' night club with DJs and loud music. It was not a party until someone put on the Jackson 5 - Rockin' Robin, ABC 123 - that was when girls couldn't decide if we loved Michael, Marlon or Jermaine more.

It was no surprise to me (or her) that she too was fascinated with this new high they call crack cocaine. We started using and selling this drug for Miami. Then I started using it for the thrill of it. I loved the way crack cocaine made me feel. It would send tingles through me. It was more enticing than the touch of any lover and it had no ill words to speak to me or of me. It felt sweet and then it allowed me to become numb. Crack cocaine became the high of choice in my diet of street pharmaceuticals. Do not take the fact that I refer to it as a diet lightly. For a diet is merely the combination of a daily intake of substance – usually food. For me, the 80's and early 90's found me on a diet of drugs that maintained my life.

What I discovered is I could take one drug to behave in one particular manner. If I needed to transform into another personality, I simply took a different drug. If I needed to just become smooth and chill, it might be just a little weed or a little swallow of the special elixir being shared at the moment. My diet was black beauties, yellow jackets, Christmas trees – speed of every strength and color, malt liquor and any other kind of liquors. They kept me moving. I didn't have to think about anything or feel anything.

In the midst of all of this, I became mommy to my second and third child. By this time I was 16 or 17 with my own apartment in the projects. A connection with someone in Daytona Housing Authority made it all possible. It also made it possible for me to do my thing at a distant eye from my mother. I thought I was grown and had it going on like nobody's business. Still, not even my own home, kept me there. The very mother I was trying to keep out of my business was pulled into deeper and deeper.

You see I had to be in the streets and on the move to get my food to feed my diet; and it was my mom who would keep the kids. She would fill in those empty moments while I filled my emptiness with a demon that had easily placed me in a gripe that I was tightening and tightening on myself. As I look back on those days, I sometimes feel the sting of what I chose to put myself through. I made deliberate choices to use my sexuality and my sensuality to entice men who had what I needed. I would leave my children, who loved their mother to life, with my mom so that I could do unspeakable things so that my body could be narcotic-aroused and then become numb.

It all became one big blurry party for me; just months and months of bodies, drugs, little bars and people who were getting high like me. If it was near the projects and I could find an escape from the reality that I really was no longer aware of then I was there. Most of the clubs near the projects were in a neighborhood called down in the Bottom. I still see the faces, the cars and attitudes that decorated the parking lots and clubs, like the bar and tables themselves. The Trop, Fullers, Georgia's Place were all down in the bottom. Most of the time I was in The Trop and Fullers Place; in same area, before you got all the way down to the bottom, was a pool hall called Blair's. We would use the bathroom and corners off from the bathrooms in all of them to smoke, if the bathrooms and corners were packed or off limit for a time, we would take our positions behind the club and let the night air help fuel the moment.

On my journey to my master, I would get up, get dressed and leave the house at 1 or 2 in the morning to walk to down to the bottom. Funny, certainly most of us have had a parent or older family member say nothing good happens in the dark; and you can't find anything but trouble hanging out in the middle of night. It is funny, in an ironic kind of way, because I would get dressed for the dark like I was getting dressed to get to my morning job. I would get dressed in the middle of the night to go down – down to the bottom. My God! I would walk through the darkest section of the Southside projects all by myself. Had the call to get high not been so strong my common sense would have prevailed in its advance warnings. Those warnings would remind me about the number of women, some drug users and some not, who had disappeared in Daytona during the era that I would take my past midnight strolls.

Some of these girls were found in the woods right off the path where I was walking; others were found raped (sometimes with foreign objects like soda bottles) and beaten to death near the pier. A strange chill moves across my body as I remember one especially frightening warning. I was walking in middle of the road, the woods and the path around me. I was alone on this road because I had not gone that far from the projects and I had checked my surroundings. Suddenly, I heard something say, "You need to turn around." I looked all around me again, there was no one. But the voice persisted, because I was still trying to get there, to my high. Something in the persistence grabbed me and the second time it spoke to me; I heard this voice say, "It is too late, go back home." As soon as the voice grew quiet I could not go any further, not because I did not want to but because physically I could not. It was like something was in the middle of the street, standing right in front of me and would not let me go pass that spot. So I finally turned around. The next day they found a girl dead on the pier. Even on the path to death, there was a power pulling me to life and am thankful that I listened to its voice; had I not, you would not have this living testament to the fact that overcoming is an option and it is the choice to live.

CHAPTER 4

I Heard My Kids Yelling

With three kids at home, the taste of crack cocaine in my system, a new man in my life – I was with baby number four. That was a wild relationship. We were both drug users and drank alcohol every day. We would fight all the time and he would cheat as much as we would fight. After that baby was born, my crack use intensified like heat from a grill on raw meat. The guy I was seeing at the time and I really began having problems and it spilled out into the streets. My mom had my first three kids and I would leave my son home with his father and disappear for days.

Enraged and high, he would come looking for me and we would be fighting in the street. Before I knew it we were being evicted. I was not paying bills because whatever money I did have or get hold to had to go to crack. I could not explain it to anyone or even to myself, but I knew that if I didn't give crack my money, he would not give me my high, my love, my peace and I would not be able to rest in the place of not feeling anything. I didn't care that I was not going to have a place to live. My kids were safe with my mom and he could be a daddy to his child. I had to get high.

The heat was turned up on me again. I was so out of control and so high one day before the eviction was final. The kids were at home with me. He and I got into a thing and I lost my mind. The details of it all are still blurry in my conscious mind; but I know that the situation got so bad that he called the police. I do not know if the call was to protect him, protect the kids or protect me – yet there they were. There presence meant nothing to me. I was so high and I was fighting. I was fighting him and I was fighting the police. They sprayed mace on me and still they couldn't get me in the car. Then I was a small girl, about five feet, seven inches tall and only about 140 pounds. Yet, at that size, not even their strength or the sting of the mace on my skin could control me. Crack had me convinced at that moment that he had my back and we were fighting all of them together. I had to be stopped though because I was going to jail, there was no deterring it this time. They pulled out their blackjacks, yet before they hit me – they, like I heard my kids yelling.

"Mommy please stop. Mommy stop. Do not hit my mommy please. Mommy please just in the car, mommy mommy please."

A moment of sanity and clarity hit me and I saw the pain and anguish pouring out in tears; I released the fight. I did not want them to see me get beat. I humbled my self long enough to be placed into the back of that police car; their voices still sound like loud piercing screams even today. Weeks after that horrible episode the eviction was evident. I had a house sale to sell everything because of it and I gave my mom some money because she had my first three kids. Somehow between the disappearing acts and the moments in jail, my fourth child ended up with a paternal aunt and out of my arms for a season.

Still, I descended deeper into hell. Each step I took, crack held me firmly around my waist escorting wonderfully into his destruction. He knew how to keep a lady's attention. I would do anything for him and I did. My disappearing days extended. I would stay with a friend who smoked crack too and I would do whatever I had to do to get the drugs and survive on the streets. I may not have been walking and standing on street corners, but read between the lines when I say I knew the guys who were selling the drugs and I did what I had to do for them and with them to get it. Crack was my pimp and I was his prostitute; what I had belonged to him as long as he would give me his time and his attention. There were times I would wonder back to my mom's house and I would hear my kids, the children that I birthed ask "who is that?" I would be like who they talking about. "Who is that?" they would ask. Then I would start talking and who they could not recognize in facial or physical appearance, they would recognize by voice. Nothing in my mind clicked then; as I wrote these words, I think something should have said HEY, YOUR OWN KIDS DO NOT RECOGNIZE YOU. What do you look like to them?

The whispers on the street were becoming louder and louder. While my sisters and brothers were fighting their own drug demons, the talk around town was all about Cyteria. Everybody seemed to know or think they knew what Pumpkin was doing and was capable of. My mom heard it all. I know in my heart of hearts she probably heard more than she ever shared with me and I know that only the hand of God could have repaired the shattered pieces caused by her children and their love of narcotics- especially me. My mom was something else. She was so concerned about her children being on the streets with drug dealers and drug users that she looked the other way while we used in her house.

When I decided to share my story, I also decided to reach out to different people who have known me at my worst and at my best, in an effort to recapture some of what I may have lost. My brother, Andrew Williams, laughed slightly when he remembered the days when I was Pumpkin. Pumpkin for him was a sweet little girl that was so skinny for so long, that people would say I was "narrow." It was only after I started putting on some weight and filling out that the name Pumpkin became mine. Andrew remembers a girl that was smart as a whip, and could catch on to things real fast – sadly, drugs were no different. I caught on to them very fast. My brother says he still remembers the girl that was always an outgoing, friendly, and a people person. He believes it was that part of my personality that led to my entrapment into abuse.

"Pumpkin," he said. "You were the same person on drugs, but the drugs just overwhelmed your personality."

"We all were shocked at first when you started using. We didn't think you would be the one to get on them. And they hit you hard! You went rock bottom." Andrew was not angry in sharing his thoughts on those times. In fact, he seemed relieved that I was still around to ask how he felt. He went on to tell me that when anyone in our family tried to talk to me it would aggravate me and make it (my drug use) worse. They were sincerely trying to rehabilitate me bud didn't really understand the kind of help I needed.

Andrew was the oldest child in the family and he was battling his own drug demons, by the time I became possessed by them. Even in his battle; he believed it was his responsibility and that he was better positioned than anybody to tell me about getting off of them and leaving them alone. My heart ached when he shared that while I dwelled in the same hell that he did, he was afraid for me.

"I didn't know how far you could fall but I knew you were falling and the bad part about it was I couldn't help you. I knew you needed help but I couldn't do it for you. I knew you couldn't do it by yourself and that was scary."

I know now that Andrew, like others who loved me thought about the possibility of finding me dead. He was horrified at the thought that his nieces and nephews, my children, would be without their mother. I am comforted, still, knowing that no matter how bad it got, they never stopped loving me.

My sister Patricia Williams and I are a year apart, so we grew up together. I asked Patricia to co-author just a little of my story. Here is what my partner in crime from the day of our birth had to say.

"Let the record show that Pumpkin and I were always close like two peas in a bucket. When you saw one you saw the other. We always had each other's back – whether we were wrong or right. As little girls growing up we were always together she was always thinner than me. Flashing back on our childhood, I recall some good memories; like playing kickball, curb ball, four square, hide and go seek, see saw, Simon says and marbles and so many others. Cyteria was always outgoing, as we grew older she proved she was not afraid of anything, she was outgoing. She was like a boy - real tough, riding motorcycles, mopeds, scooter bikes – in the 70's it was unusual for girls to do that. That tomboy phase did not last long, she became just as interested in boys as I was and we both experienced childhood sweethearts at the same time and even became pregnant within a year of each other.

Becoming young, unwed mothers also meant we then had a source of income through the welfare system. This provided us with an opportunity to move in together – the two of us and our babies. We shared an apartment in the South Street Projects – the same place we grew up in and where our mother still lived. Pumpkin was 16 and I was 15.

We shared many things in our apartment home, including our first getting drunk experience. It was a bottle of 80 proof Vodka. We got drunk, fell asleep, and woke up throwing up. This apartment away from our mother's eyes opened the door for more drugs, alcohol and clubbing. We were still in high school, but we also still going to the clubs. Thursday night was ladies' night and we were always in the place, so that meant sometimes on Friday morning we were late for school because we would miss the school bus and have to take Voltran to school. Our mother would always walk down the block to our apartment to wake us up and make sure we went to school. Her passion was strong; all of her children were going to finish school. Pumpkin was so tied and tangled up in the street life that she paid the price of not graduating with her class in 1981. I went on to graduate with my class in 1982; it was a bittersweet celebration because Cyteria was not there. It broke my heart but I understood that the drugs, alcohol and street life had taken over.

I and Cyteria eventually started taking Black Beauties; sometimes we would take the capsules apart and snort. Then one of Cy's boyfriend's sisters would come over and bring powdered cocaine and we started snorting that too. It was not a big deal for us, because we figured it didn't really spark again inside. I got involved with this guy who was freebasing but Cy didn't know I was freebasing with him. This was during the time people discovered that Richard Pryor was freebasing. Put on a pipe with marijuana or with acid, rolling the crack in a joint. The same sister, Brenda Gail, that introduced us to marijuana at age 12, introduced Cy to crack. I do not believe she knew the affect it would have on Cy's life; she was in bondage too.

Shortly after that Cy got introduced to crack on a pipe/on a stem. We found out she was doing it. The addiction got so bad for both of us that we would wake up knowing that with money or without money we were going to make something happen. I was the one who was the go getter I did a lot of selling and buying and Cy would be with me. Like if someone came thru and wanted me to sell for them, I would sell for a percentage of the drugs and give her some. She would never get high on the streets; instead, she would go somewhere she could get high privately.

When she had her youngest son, she wanted to quit so bad, we were always together a lot during that pregnancy but every once in awhile. Although I was still getting high, I had more control because I had started putting the crack pressed down in cigarettes. The wakeup call for Pumpkin came when she got pregnant with her last son. The crack demon was riding her even stronger by then and her son was taken away from her and given to his father; because she had crack in her blood stream when he was born. She had the willpower to fight then. She attended Alcoholic Anonymous, Narcotics Anonymous and other treatment and parenting programs. She did whatever was necessary to get her son back. After staying clean for years, she knew that she need something more – something was still missing."

What pain it brings to my spirit to know that I was so in love with crack, that my actions made me abandon a special moment for my sister. I was getting high and I had to be out there getting it wherever it was. My mom would look for us, I remember times she would specifically look for one of my brothers and for me. She would either bring us something to eat or convince us to go back to the house to eat. Then she would open her heart and let us stay. Still we were hard core users and her home became nothing more than a drug den. That she could not and would not tolerate; her grandkids were there and she was going to protect them. We broke her heart again. The very children she raised and showed compassion for even in their deliberate wrong; she now had to tell to leave her house.

So leave I did and I managed to find favor again and ended up in another apartment in the projects. In my own space again, I was positioned to dance however crack told me to.

CHAPTER 5

You Got To Think About Your Babies

I cannot say I remember the exact moment or even the time period; but at some point I realized that not only had I become a crack fiend, but I had pulled my family into the abyss that is drug addiction. Surely there were people around us that thought my mom was wrong for allowing her adult children – who were using drugs – to spend any time in her house. It is my belief in the crevices of my heart that she did it, because she wanted to assure to some degree that we were okay. I believe, that like me, my mom did not want to hear that one of her babies - that her Pumpkin - was found dead in some crack house or alley.

My mom loved her kids. She gave her whole self and her whole life to her kids. She was always willing to do whatever she needed to for us. That meant she would rather us be at her house, in our home on drugs than in the streets. I have an extra dose of respect for my mother; for no matter what people would come and tell her about me or about what I was doing in the streets, she loved me and kept her arms open to me. No matter what she never said she was embarrassed or ashamed. She never made condemning remarks like, "you will never get off the drugs," or "you will never be anything but an addict." She never talked down to us. She would however feed me her brand of tough love.

"Pumpkin baby... You got to think about your babies. They need their mama." She would say, "You need to make some decisions about your life, about your kids." She had a unique and special love.

In some quiet moments, I often think about what my mother must have seen when she looked at me. I recall sometimes, I would see her face; how she would hold the tears in and try not to let her fear show. Still, I would hear the pain in her voice. I imagine that with every word she spoke to me, there was a prayer she uttered behind it. Her movements at times seemed slow and heavy. My God the weight of the burden I must have placed on her shoulders. The terror of a drug monster, one who carried razor blades hidden on her body for the seemingly ever present invitation to fight; and beyond that was the trouble of raising grandkids when she should have been resting.

My mom was the kind of person you could tell anything; still when I got pregnant the first time, I was terrified to break that news to her. Someone else did it for me. There was this neighborhood clinic just outside of the projects, which meant there were all kinds of roving eyes. A pair of those eyes happened to see me and my baby daddy there; while they shared news of our sighting they could not confirm anything else. I left that task to my boyfriend.

While mom would tear apart hell for her children, she was nobody's push over. She was a typical old school mother, who set her rules and boundaries, and when you crossed them – you dealt with the circumstances. She was that mother that would take care of your bad behavior moment immediately with whatever she could get her hands on. I remember this particular occasion, where I had grown angry about something. In my anger I threw a container of marbles on the floor where she was sweeping. The next thing I knew, she and that broom were adjusting my attitude. Surely, you have heard comedian Eddie Murphy talk about his mother's disciplining ability with a shoe; with my momma it could be a shoe or an empty vegetable can, if we happened to cut the fool while she was cooking dinner.

On another occasion, there was a weekly school dance, oh how my sister and I wanted to go. My mom had already said no several times. No, was not the answer we wanted to hear, so when we assumed everyone in the house was distracted, we snuck out the bedroom window. Knowing that when or if we got caught there would be mama to deal with, I assured my sister I would take her whooping for her. So out the window we went. When we came back there was mama and she decided we would each take our own consequence. What a lesson I have should have learned; you take the consequence for the trouble you purposely walk into – even when you think you know and can handle the outcome.

This sorrow grabs me. It is a sorrow that comes from thinking about the nights my mother must have laid her head on her pillow, with the thoughts of what her child was doing in the streets. I can help but consider that she must have wailed before God at what had become of the child she once cradled to her bosom and who was the child being controlled, and happily so, by a demon. It was a control so strong that there was even an occasion I spoke to my mom like she was nothing more than another simple street woman. I was high, my mom and I got into an argument about my kids and I had the audacity to curse her. She read me from A to Z.

My mother died in 2008 after a long and serious illness. Her sick days were made easy by the caring attention of her children, especially by the loving concern of my baby sister. She had always been there to help bear the weight of what some of her siblings put on mama and I am grateful to her for that. I am also grateful to God that I had the chance to apologize to her before she died. I am even more grateful that she saw her daughter clean and the love of her mother being restored to her children. I miss her ability to burn (cook extremely well) in the kitchen; yet her talent for the same lives in my hands and so her love is stirred in each pot every time I cook.

One of the most notorious and well known drug dealers and gangsters in Daytona Beach, Florida was the man I knew as daddy. My parents were not together a lot. Daddy was a womanizer and a gambler on top of his illegal entrepreneurship. There were times I would go to his house and the drugs would be laid out on plates like a holiday buffet. When crack hit Daytona daddy's business expanded and so did his money.

My daddy was something mean. He was not the kind of man you could even look at funny; like father like daughter I guess. When we were in school and he was there; he ran a tight ship. It ran like clock work - you came home from school by a specified time, you did your homework before anything else, you went out side for a brief time, then it was time for dinner, a bath, watch one TV show and then bed.

As we grew older, we learned that the mean and hard streak that was synonymous with my father came from a traumatic event. My grandmother was stabbed to death by a lover. Enraged with himself for not being there to save her, his whole approach to life became bathed in anger and resentment. He did prison time at Raiford for killing a man. While we never fully knew the details, just the rumblings in the neighborhood; we used to go visit. How happy all of us would be to just see him and take possession of the gifts he would have made for us - pocketbooks and other things.

Daddy was a bad boy. It was the affection of this bad boy that led me to the arms of so many others. That was not my father's intention I am sure nor was it something I can say I consciously decided to look for – the bad boy. It is simply the fact that I never got that special daddy attention I so wanted and so needed, not the way I saw him entrust it to others including my sister. When my descent began, my father was keenly aware of what

I was becoming; yet like everyone else how to rescue me was beyond his grasp. His daughter was becoming one of the biggest consumers of the thing that made him wealthy; still the addictive side of the business was not where his smarts were. He had no choice but to leave me to fall deeper into despair.

For a period of time, my sister was selling drugs for him and doing other things for him in his business. Often I was with her. We both got into a major fight one night with a street woman that clearly hated us with a passion. My sister and I were arrested. To my surprise, my father bailed my sister out immediately but left me in jail for 29 days. The charge was battery. I was devastated. When I was released I confronted him about his decision to give one daughter freedom and leave another in jail. His response came in a very matter of fact way, "I wanted you to dry out so I left you there." My devastation grew; you see my sister was on drugs too. This is the kind of rejection I used to go through and came accustomed to in other intimate relationships. All daddy wanted was what he wanted and he used whoever he needed to get it, including his daughter.

I think my father did the best he could. I honestly believe he did what he knew – some people you simply cannot teach to love and they cannot love. The streets of Daytona would often buzz with little things like Pumpkin was a druggie because her daddy was a dealer. I do not place blame on my father for anything I became. I cannot blame him for my choice to become an addict or an alcoholic. You see if I blamed him for any part of my time in hell, then I leave a degree of power in someone else's hands. God snatched me from the deepest pits and therefore I give no one on earth the power to return me to that previous address. Before my father died, I had entered rehab the first time, and so I take some comfort in knowing that he transcended from this life having reconciled with me and at least knowing that my liberty from addiction was possible.

As a daughter I had to struggle with the hurt, pain and disappointment that I handed my parents like a well-wrapped Christmas present. I struggled with how their hearts, especially my mother's, must have bled from my choices. Still that struggle was nothing in comparison to what I presented to my children. My five beautiful children each experienced their mom's world of drugs in a different facet. It is an experience they never asked for and I am certain if they could they would wish it away.

CHAPTER 6

A Child Destined For Something

"In all honesty, my sister and I grew up without our mother. This is a major disservice to us. For I know our lives would be different (better) if we had our mother the way she is now growing up. I would trade all my successes in life to go back in time and have Reverend Cyteria Freeman as my mother." Treniqua Anderson, my oldest child.

My first daughter was born when I was 15. My baby and I experienced a wonderful life together; we were after all growing up together. That life lasted for about five years before the drugs would become a regular visitor at the family home. While I played in hell, my daughter and my other kids were being raised by mom and a younger sister. When she hit those delicate pre-teen and teen years, our tears became intense.

My kids' attempts to be at home with me were horrible. They used to call my house, "the house of pain." While they craved my maternal attention, the bulk of what I gave them was an introduction to the party life. Our project castle was all about parties – parties all the time, beer and liquor drinking and drugs. She had no respect for me. Things got so bad between us that she was talking back and became very rebellious. Our relationship became bitter, I made a lot of promises that I didn't keep.

This was a child that was destined for something and I believe she knew it. She longed for a mother who could not only see her greatness but could help her get to it. She was an athlete. She ran track, played basketball and volleyball – she won numerous awards in all of them and academically. I was never clean enough to go to her games or her award ceremonies.

When my second daughter was born, it gave the first daughter back up, especially as they grew older. They would link up and come against me, typically when I did one of my reappearing acts and try to be a parent who could discipline a child. This child was a fighter; she (as I look back) became the protector of the two girls. She would throw up a wall and make it clear I was not to come through it. She would throw everything in my face - the clubbing, the partying and the drugs.

She was hurt. She, like her sister, had to be thrust into a stricter world, with my mom's rules. When I was able to be their mother, our home was fun, we were the girls! They were used to being with me cooking dinner, cleaning up and playing games. Then suddenly the mask of the monster never came off and I would not even go to a PTA meeting because I didn't want to embarrass them. Every one in the neighborhood knew I was on drugs; that however did not mean I had to present it like a prize at my children's school.

The girls had a right to be full of anger. I had given them so many reasons. Little girl birthday celebrations would become big girl liquor bashes. What would start out as nothing more than spending the night with grandma while mommy went out, would end up being living with grandma while mommy played the disappearing game for days on end. My second daughter was clear in her sentiment, she felt I chose drugs over them and I have to say for a long season I did.

"I never heard things at school about what you were doing initially. School was a place where I thought I was safe. As time went on my attitude changed about school and learning. Learning became the second main objective to me and trouble was the first. Wearing holes in my shoes, dirty clothes, hair nappy, and no supplies to do my work made me not interested and I didn't want to be there."

Shawntrell says she learned about my relationship with the drug fiend from a neighbor in the projects. This neighbor, who also was a drug dealer, invited her into his car. When she refused, he apparently made a grand announcement to my child (in front of everyone), that I was on crack and that I sold stuff to get high. Rather than ask me, and honestly, I am not sure how I would have responded, she decided to do her own investigation. In that investigation, Shawntrell tells me that she would notice that the handles on bleach and milk bottles were missing.

One night, I am sure long after I thought she and the others were asleep, she found me in the bathroom getting high. It was one of my favorite places to get high at home. Shawntrell remembers peeping through the door and there I sat with a self-made pipe (constructed of the missing handles) to my mouth and fire at the other end. I was smoking crack. For Shawntrell, that was a turning moment, the moment she began to hate who I was. She didn't respect me as a mother or as an authority figure. My daughter believes that I was jealous of their relationship with my mother; she believes I hated that relationship. I knew that if it were not for my mother and my sister, my children would have had to raise themselves.

While, our relationship has crossed many bridges towards healing; my youngest daughter still remembers the days when she didn't want to be seen with the mother who looked like a monster. She wanted nothing to do with the mother who she recalls as being a thief who would steal and sell their school clothes and shoes; and even their Christmas presents one year. That mother was the one she wanted to flee from and instead live with a normal family with regular problems like paying bills and where to take vacation.

My daughters experienced so many things that contributed to who they are as women without my presence. They wanted their mom to be there, my mom did a terrific job with them but they wanted THEIR mom. My spirit groans at what they encountered from class mates (after that grand announcement in the midst of the projects) who knew I was on drugs. They heard the names. The names were probably hurled at them daily. "Your mama is a drug head, rock monster, crack fiend." I know that it bothered them and probably ripped into their hearts with each hurl.

My first son was my third child. Interestingly, while I did not do drugs during my pregnancy with him, he was a problem child. He was very hyper, wouldn't sit still. I literally had to go to school with this child to help control his behavior. It is my belief these problems were generational, his father was that way – hyper, moving and doing things constantly. Plus he was the offspring of two people with horrible tempers.

While he didn't see the full monster that my daughters did, he unfortunately did witness her capabilities to some degree. While my daughters dealt with the rejection of their mother's presence in their own way, my son took a hard turn. He started going to jail a lot as a juvenile … selling drugs, using drugs he sadly was following in his parents' footsteps. During his struggle, I had come through one round of hell long enough to be there for him; and with each court date he knew his mother would be there. Because of a merciful God, he is now a loveable and loving man. It brings a smile to my spirit to hear him say he loves me and there is nothing I could have done to embarrass him.

By the time I had child number four, a second son, I had really stopped showing up. No one would know where I was for weeks on end. I would leave him with his father in search of that great high that I could not catch again. His father used to come in the streets looking for me. His father was not on drugs, he was a DJ who drank heavily. I had abandoned them and they were evicted. Even now, I am grieved, because for the love of the high; my son ended up with an aunt and I can not even tell you how or really when. I speculate my mother just could not take in another child; but I honestly am not sure. For the love of the high, my son was not only taken away from me but from his sisters and brother as well. We were torn asunder and I was too high to notice it. I would try to visit him from time to time much to the dismay of his father and aunt. He was my child though and I was determined to see him. Finally that game grew old with me. There was never a court custody order, so one day I picked him up and took him home. Our relationship is still mending, but it is mending and not asunder. We are both in the Lord, and we have respect for each other.

My fifth and final child is the hardest to face. It was a crack pregnancy. There was not a time I carried this child in my womb that I was not high. I was so high and drunk that the day I went into labor and I did not realize I was. When I got to the hospital, my son was born in 15 minutes. I recall the doctor asking if I was drunk or high. I told him that I had been binging for days. I would binge for three or four days and then I would crash for days like I was in a coma.

He was born with very mild complications, but nothing that said this was a child that had been growing on a diet of drugs and alcohol. They placed him on medications to address the complications. I had given birth to a crack baby. In the state of Florida, that meant I had given birth to a child they were compelled to protect. Child protective services stepped in within days and took him. My mother was devastated and suddenly I realized that it was all out of control. I had one child temporarily taken from me and now another was in state custody, not even my mother's love would be his. My mother did finally end up with him and I went to Stewart-Marchman, a drug treatment center. My mother would bring him to see me and his little laugh would make the whole word feel so attainable.

She would tell me, "Pumpkin, this baby loves you. When he goes too many days without seeing you he won't even eat."

When I held my son in my arms again after child protective services took him in me, there was no evidence that crack cocaine had been in his system. I was amazed and so were the doctors and my family. He grew up like any normal child – healthy, happy and no sense of wanting for crack cocaine. I remember his favorite juice – apple. I was very protective of him because of what I knew about babies born with crack in their systems. What I did not know was that God was in control from the beginning of his life, even at conception. It is Jeremiah 1:5 that says, "Before I formed thee in the belly, I knew thee and before thou came forth out of the womb I sanctified thee." My son is a child of God. He is grown up to be a responsible young man.

The restoration that God can provide is wondrous and peaceable. While talking about that period in our lives is painful for many of my children, they are all proud of who I am today. It is mind blowing to them to see and know what there mom was and what I am today and they are not ashamed. They remember the mother who used to go in the bathroom a lot and do drugs. They see the mother that now goes into a prayer closet and accept the liberty of Christ. God has done such a work with my kids and me, that I was honored and trusted to raise my granddaughter while my eldest child went to college. Isn't that something? The mother she could not even trust to tell her the truth, she entrusted enough to take care of her child.

My grandkids have seen the articles that have appeared in The News Journal. The headline WELCOME TO CRACK CORNER; A SIX-YEAR JOURNEY: ONE WOMAN'S STRUGGLE, grabs their attention. It is important to me that I do whatever I can to keep them from making the choice for drugs. More than public service announcements, my story, the story of the woman they call Nana is the greatest reason not to. So I sit down and talk to them in an age appropriate way about what I did and why I did it. I talk to them about how Nana was a bad girl and being bad like that was not good at all. I talk to them about the fact that if God did not want me to be here to love them and to do His work, I would probably be dead. I tell my daughters to lean and depend on God, and to seek whatever services you need to, but always talk to your kids open, honestly and candidly.

"The Lord works in mysterious ways. It may seem like a cliché, but I know from my own life that this is the most factual statement in Christianity. I got pregnant my freshman year of college. So that I could continue school without any hindrance, my mom volunteered to quit her job and take care of my daughter. This was one of the greatest gifts of my life. The mother who had not been there for me was able and willing to be there for me and my child in this magnitude. Had she not found God and straightened up her life, I would not have trusted her with my most precious gift. Because I witnessed her transformation myself, I was able to allow her to help raise my daughter. Even though she had changed, I was very apprehensive in the beginning. With time, my mother's commitment put my soul at ease. Allowing my mom to raise my daughter still is to this day the hardest thing I ever have done. This situation with my pregnancy brought my mom and me closer. I built a relationship with her that had never existed before my daughter's birth. I feel that this was God's plan all along."

I read my eldest daughter's words and I am filled with joy. It had to be a merciful and forgiving God that would allow me to love and raise my granddaughter in a way that I could not raise her mother, because of the demonic influence of drugs. My first four kids really saw the beast that I became – the disfigured face, the crazy eyes and the funny looking skin. Sometimes I would come home after being out there for weeks, they would just look at me like who is that. When I got clean, there were so many things that I regretted. I could not forgive myself, and I am still stunned that drugs had become so serious for me that I would do my kids the way that I did. I had to really learn to forgive myself. I had to learn to forgive my kids for lashing out in anger and desiring the lashing to hurt me severely.

I still feel like I took something from them and I did. I took part of their lives. I gave them so many horrible things to be worried about so young in life. They had to figure out what was going on with their mom, what was going to happen to their mom and whether a knock at the door was someone coming with the news - "Pumpkin is dead." Nana was a bad girl. Nana is now a delivered, liberated and forgiven girl; who is grateful to God she is.

I am grateful to God that the daughter who at one point, didn't want to be seen with me, would write these words: "Our relationship now is better then before. It took awhile to get it here but it is better. I hated my mom for a long time for putting me and my sister and brothers through that kind of devastation. I didn't want anything to do with her for a long time. I had to figure it out and let it go for me and my children because I was still holding on to the past of all the hurt, the lies, and the shame. If I never would've let it go I would've stay depressed for longer than I did. Now, I do not think about those days, I know that it was a struggle and I thank God for keeping her. If it were not for Him, she would have never found her ability to do great things."

Treniqua sees the God in me as well and I hope the very image of Christ in me is mirrored in them daily. "I witnessed my mom enter rehab, stay clean for a little while, then find drugs again. I feel that her deliverance was maintained after the last rehab trial because she discovered Jesus Christ. My mom talks about God habitually. Whenever you turn to her for advice, she will recite a scripture in the Bible to help you with your current situation. My mom lives, breathes, and sleeps God's Holy word."

CHAPTER 7

A Prayer I Mimic

One of the things my mother prayed for during her final days was that the relationships among her children would be restored. It is a prayer I mimic to this day. We are all not close; I think it is less because of the severity of my addiction and more of our basic adult differences. Still, I was the epitome of the black sheep. I was one that had the most kids and started at such an early age. I was the one that was very blatant and wild with my drug use. I think most of them are still ashamed of me.

So now those of us who were considered the outcasts stick together. The ones that felt like they were better, or in an upper class, do not really associate with us. There were times we would go weeks or months without talking to each other. That was not the prayer my mother placed before a God who had already assured her restoration is possible.

We had our struggles. My oldest sister and oldest brother smoked crack. Because I was not in my proper place as a mom, my baby sister had to help raise my kids and so being the one with five kids and mom having to take care of them that put a lot of strain on my family. The sister under me in age used and sold drugs; though she was more of a functioning addict than I. She and I have always been close, we would fight together and fight other people and we fought our way through addiction. Now we have a ministry called Victoriously Overcoming; it is a substance abuse radio broadcast ministry. We walk the street evangelizing.

When the invitation to finally be free came to me after the birth of my fifth child, I found a passage of scripture that I would read and read and read. I felt like I had to absorb it so that it oozed like sweat from my pores. That passage is Romans 8.

¹There is therefore now no condemnation to them which are in Christ Jesus, who walk not after the flesh, but after the Spirit.

²For the law of the Spirit of life in Christ Jesus hath made me free from the law of sin and death.

³For what the law could not do, in that it was weak through the flesh, God sending his own Son in the likeness of sinful flesh, and for sin, condemned sin in the flesh:

⁴That the righteousness of the law might be fulfilled in us, who walk not after the flesh, but after the Spirit.

⁵For they that are after the flesh do mind the things of the flesh; but they that are after the Spirit the things of the Spirit.

⁶For to be carnally minded is death; but to be spiritually minded is life and peace.

⁷Because the carnal mind is enmity against God: for it is not subject to the law of God, neither indeed can be.

⁸So then they that are in the flesh cannot please God.

⁹But ye are not in the flesh, but in the Spirit, if so be that the Spirit of God dwells in you. Now if any man have not the Spirit of Christ, he is none of his.

¹⁰And if Christ be in you, the body is dead because of sin; but the Spirit is life because of righteousness.

¹¹But if the Spirit of him that raised up Jesus from the dead dwell in you, he that raised up Christ from the dead shall also quicken your mortal bodies by his Spirit that dwelleth in you.

¹²Therefore, brethren, we are debtors, not to the flesh, to live after the flesh.

¹³For if ye live after the flesh, ye shall die: but if ye through the Spirit do mortify the deeds of the body, ye shall live.

¹⁴For as many as are led by the Spirit of God, they are the sons of God.

¹⁵For ye have not received the spirit of bondage again to fear; but ye have received the Spirit of adoption, whereby we cry, Abba, Father.

¹⁶The Spirit itself beareth witness with our spirit, that we are the children of God:

¹⁷And if children, then heirs; heirs of God, and joint-heirs with Christ; if so be that we suffer with him, that we may be also glorified together.

¹⁸For I reckon that the sufferings of this present time are not worthy to be compared with the glory which shall be revealed in us.

¹⁹For the earnest expectation of the creature waiteth for the manifestation of the sons of God.

²⁰For the creature was made subject to vanity, not willingly, but by reason of him who hath subjected the same in hope,

²¹Because the creature itself also shall be delivered from the bondage of corruption into the glorious liberty of the children of God.

²²For we know that the whole creation groaneth and travaileth in pain together until now.

²³And not only they, but ourselves also, which have the first fruits of the Spirit, even we ourselves groan within ourselves, waiting for the adoption, to wit, the redemption of our body.

²⁴For we are saved by hope: but hope that is seen is not hope: for what a man seeth, why doth he yet hope for?

²⁵But if we hope for that we see not, then do we with patience wait for it.

²⁶Likewise the Spirit also helpeth our infirmities: for we know not what we should pray for as we ought: but the Spirit itself maketh intercession for us with groanings which cannot be uttered.

²⁷And he that searcheth the hearts knoweth what is the mind of the Spirit, because he maketh intercession for the saints according to the will of God.

²⁸And we know that all things work together for good to them that love

God, to them who are the called according to his purpose.

[29]For whom he did foreknow, he also did predestinate to be conformed to the image of his Son, that he might be the firstborn among many brethren.

[30]Moreover whom he did predestinate, them he also called: and whom he called, them he also justified: and whom he justified, them he also glorified.

[31]What shall we then say to these things? If God be for us, who can be against us?

[32]He that spared not his own Son, but delivered him up for us all, how shall he not with him also freely give us all things?

[33]Who shall lay any thing to the charge of God's elect? It is God that justifieth.

[34]Who is he that condemneth? It is Christ that died, yea rather, that is risen again, who is even at the right hand of God, who also maketh intercession for us.

[35]Who shall separate us from the love of Christ? Shall tribulation, or distress, or persecution, or famine, or nakedness, or peril, or sword?

[36]As it is written, for thy sake we are killed all the day long; we are accounted as sheep for the slaughter.

[37]Nay, in all these things we are more than conquerors through him that loved us.

CHAPTER 8

Do Not Let Me Die Like This

Even in our descent into the gates of hell, God will reach out to you and spare your life. For while the fire burns us, it is nothing more than light tickles to Him. It has no power and no sting to the Most High God. Through my dance with the devil, God's hand was forever upon me. So many people I grew up with got hooked on the same crack introduced to me. Some became prostitutes on the corners, the bodies hanging free for the advantage of anyone and sometimes all that anyone needed was a five dollar bill. Here I was set up in every possible situation where any of a long list of sexually transmitted diseases could have and should have invaded my body. My actions and my inability to rationally surmise that I should use protection; are a text book case scenario for contracting syphilis, gonorrhea, HIV/AIDS and/or herpes. Yet I did not. God's hand was on me.

Some died and were found with the fluids from their bodies oozing; the only way the others high around them knew they had – as they say – crossed over. We would mourn long enough to decide to get high to forget the dead. That could have easily been me. There were times I would be so high I thought if I went to sleep - I would never wake up. So I would grab hold of that fear and use it to keep me awake for days on end. I would pray and cry in the midst of the fatigue and high state of mind, "God please do not let me die like this! I do not want to be one of these people." But like a lot of users, that death fear would pass with another light of the pipe. We simply kept it pushing.

So often I think about the nights I would walk through the path in the projects, with nothing but the moon lighting the way. I did not always hear that voice of warning. I knew it was dangerous. I knew that the deeper I walked into it the more likely I could be pulled into the woods. I knew that every step I took through that pass, I put myself in the position for one of the neighborhood kids to come through there the next morning and find Pumpkin exposed with insects crawling over my body. I knew that it would have been real easy for the police to just say another crack head was found dead and it would be a neighbor who had to tell my mother and my children. I was just so tired, too tired and too strung out to seek a safer route; instead I would walk through there and pray the whole time. I would walk and pray - that is what I did.

CHAPTER 9

These Drugs Have Taken Over My Body

For the next great high, I would put my self into situations where death was probable. There was this guy, a known drug dealer near the projects and the bottom, I approached him about drugs. Before I knew it, I was in his home just on the outskirts of the projects and I was in trouble. Like so much of that time, because I was in the midst of narcotic ecstasy, the details are fuzzy, but the reality was I was being held hostage. He would lock me in a room and then lock the doors on the outside of the house so I could not get out. For days he kept me there and I was sure he was going to kill me to keep me from telling anyone. I begged. He ignored me. I pleaded. He ignored me. One name however scared him. I said to him, somebody knows I'm missing by now and that something is not right. If somebody gets to my daddy and tells him you are dead for sure. At first he was not impressed.

"Just who is your punk daddy? I do not care nothing about your daddy?"

He was not moved, that is, until I threw my daddy's name at him, slapping him across the face with it. He didn't even know it, but finally my father had given me the kind of attention I wanted and this time it saved my life. I got out of that house and went to get high. I do not know what happened to him; I just went back to living the life that was closing in on me.

When I would leave the streets, I would go back to an empty apartment. I would stumble into the bathroom in the apartment and glance at the image of a creature in the mirror. I would realize that creature was me. I would cry behind closed doors and say, "Lord do not let no one see me like this, do not let me die looking like this. Do not ever let my kids see me like this." I would get by myself and look in the mirror and I would say, "Lord, these drugs have taken control of my body and they are living in me." I would stay away on purpose, believing my absence was better for them. When I came to know God's full deliverance; I thought about the Word of God that warns us a one demon goes and gets seven others in his inhabitation. The longer I committed adultery with the demonic crack, the more my countenance became the likeness of the imp that controlled me for the moment.

One morning I was up getting high, a very normal routine for me; it was an especially bright morning and as much as I can remember about it, it was equally still. I sat in the room getting high and suddenly the brightness of that room hid beneath darkness. The room got dark. This was not the dim mood that moves in temporarily when the clouds move in front of the sun; this was utter darkness. It was as though night had come at a moment's notice. I looked around the dark room, trying to figure out if I was tripping. Had I gotten a bad cut of the rock or was it laced with some hallucinogenic? In the darkness, all I could see was snakes; snakes on the walls, on the curtains and on the door. There were snakes on everything in the room where I sat. Some were alive and others dead but they were all jabbing at me. They were all coming after me. There was a light around me but I was terrified and I heard something say if you have enough faith to open that door you will not have to worry about drugs anymore. Somehow I opened the door and when I came to my senses I was on the other side of the projects, but facing my apartment there was no one around. I ran back to my apartment. And I told God if he took the drugs out of my mouth that I would do whatever he wanted me to.

JEREMIAH 8: 17-22 KJV

[17]For, behold, I will send serpents, cockatrices, among you, which will not be charmed, and they shall bite you, saith the LORD.

[18]When I would comfort myself against sorrow, my heart is faint in me.

[19]Behold the voice of the cry of the daughter of my people because of

them that dwell in a far country: Is not the LORD in Zion? Is not her king in her? Why have they provoked me to anger with their graven images, and with strange vanities?

[20]The harvest is past, the summer is ended, and we are not saved.

[21]For the hurt of the daughter of my people am I hurt; I am black; astonishment hath taken hold on me.

[22]Is there no balm in Gilead; is there no physician there? Why then is not the health of the daughter of my people recovered?

CHAPTER 10

Crazy Stuff Professing My Deliverance

I had a reputation for something else on the streets. Aside from the hidden razors, the fight and the drugs, I was known for always having something to say about God. I was famous for praying when I got high. I remember a time I had been up all night getting high. This was an especially good high, the kind that did not come often. So I am floating and feeling lovely, when something in me started crying out to God. I was crying out asking Him to take the taste of the drugs out of my mouth. I promised if He took it for good, I would never come back.

I would do crazy stuff like professing my deliverance while I was high and a battle raged between heaven and hell over my life. I would tell drug dealers, "One day soon, you watch - I am not going to buy your drugs anymore. I am going be able to tell you about a God who loves me and you too. I would tell people in the crack house, one day I'm not going to be in this crack house with you." I would tell them God is going to save me. God was speaking through me and for His glory even in a drug-induced stupor.

I was already walking in God's promises to heal and deliver found in the book of Matthew.

MATTHEW 8:16

When the even was come, they brought unto him many that were possessed with devils: and he cast out the spirits with his word, and healed all that were sick:

MATTHEW 4

[23]And Jesus went about all Galilee, teaching in their synagogues, and preaching the gospel of the kingdom, and healing all manner of sickness and all manner of disease among the people.

[24]And his fame went throughout all Syria: and they brought unto him all sick people that were taken with divers diseases and torments, and those which were possessed with devils, and those which were lunatic, and those that had the palsy; and he healed them.

I learned something about God and about His deliverance. You have to participate in that deliverance. The first time I went into treatment I missed that valuable lesson. You see the first time I went into treatment I was depending too much on me and not enough on God. I figured I had it all together. I had done what they asked me to and I had been clean for eight months. That time in treatment had dug up some stuff in me. I had to face the hard reality of being the kind of woman that would feed her unborn child crack cocaine. I had endured the name calling from a child protective services worker who told me she was going to do everything she could to keep my last child from me. She said I was a horrible mother and I did not deserve that child. There was no way I was going to become a monster again.

I lied. A year and half of being clean, I felt my "strength". I wanted to show everyone that I was bigger than the drugs. I wanted to prove that I could still be around the users and the dealers and not smoke crack. I fooled myself. It started with sharing a soda or two with some of the old gang. Sharing a soda led to sharing a beer and one drink here and there; I quickly graduated again to the head of the class and for five more years cracked and I tangoed once again.

After the ordeal with the snakes reality hit me in the face. Reality said, "You are getting ready to not only die mentally and spiritually but physically." That situation frightened me so bad, even thinking about it now it is breathtaking. I was totally out of control. I could not distinguish between right and wrong.

The cocaine beast is so crafty and manipulative that you can not figure out what he looks like. The longer he manipulates you, the more you assimilate and the more you start to look like part of that beast's family. When you become that demon then sadly you have no problem making your bed in hell.

When that bed in hell however, becomes uncomfortable and lumpy and unfit to sleep in; you begin to look for a pillow that is not a rock; but is deliverance and divine comfort. I know that God pulled me off of that bed of affliction and put me in a place of therapy and on a road to recovery. My sister Patricia writes about that time and I am honored to share her words.

"The last time she went to treatment there was something different about her. Our father had passed away April 6, 1990; Cy was in treatment, she wrote a poem while there and she was strong enough to read it at daddy's funeral. She had always thought she would not amount to anything. She would curse my dad because he was not always the father he should have been. After Cy did that poem it seemed she was getting stronger.

"When Pumpkin realized that there was something missing in her life that had nothing to do with drugs, she found it. It was after attending a funeral of some young men we knew growing up. Bishop Derek T. Triplett, Pastor of Hope Fellowship Ministries in Daytona Beach, preached a eulogy that changed something in her. My sister has never been the same. That message literally changed her life and she accepted Jesus Christ as her personal Savior. She continued to grow and develop into a mighty, powerful woman of God. She received her minister's license in August of 2001, the 12th exactly – my birthday. Her life has taken wings and the sky is not even the limit to what God wants to do in her life."

From there I become part of the intercessory prayer ministry and became a minister-in-training and finally an ordained minister. My sister and I went on to start a radio ministry and I have served and loved God with everything in me from that moment until now.

CHAPTER 11

I Began To cast Out The Cocaine Demon

After five years of a second trip to hell; I felt the weariness on my bones. I felt the chains that I had carried for eight years rattling every time I moved and even breathed. I was tired. I was tired of getting high. I was tired of waiting for someone or the drugs to kill me or me to kill somebody. I wanted to stop feeling like I was the crud at the very bottom of the barrel. I was finally scared that my children would never forgive me or love me. In my mind, heart and spirit I knew that if I got up and headed towards one more hit, I would be dead. I was convinced of it. So, instead, I started prophesying to myself.

I began to cast out the cocaine demon. I began to pray for me. I became determined to believe that if God set me free I would be free indeed. In February 1995, I entered Stewart-Marchman's in-patient program. I had to confront everything that I had done to myself, to my children and to my family. I had to admit that I could not do it alone. For me, not doing it alone meant doing it with and because of God.

MATTHEW 9

[16]No man putteth a piece of new cloth unto an old garment, for that which is put in to fill it up taketh from the garment, and the rent is made worse. [17]Neither do men put new wine into old bottles: else the bottles break, and the wine runneth out, and the bottles perish: but they put new wine into new bottles, and both are preserved.

JOHN 8

[31]Then said Jesus to those Jews which believed on him, If ye continue in my word, then are ye my disciples indeed;
[32]And ye shall know the truth, and the truth shall make you free.
[33]They answered him, We be Abraham's seed, and were never in bondage

to any man: how sayest thou, Ye shall be made free?

³⁴Jesus answered them, Verily, verily, I say unto you, Whosoever committeth sin is the servant of sin.

³⁵And the servant abideth not in the house for ever: but the Son abideth ever.

³⁶If the Son therefore shall make you free, ye shall be free indeed.

In 1995, the demon had no choice but to flee. I had made up my mind for God. I had decided that I was going to accept every prayer that my mother had lifted for me and I knew that God was honoring every scream to help me that I had ever yelled out – even though I was high during most of those pleas. At night, headaches and bad dreams would wrestle with me. The dreams would taunt me, "you are an addict, you can't get off drug, you are scum, you are low, come on back and get high." The demon forgot that I am a fighter and I fought back every night until there were no headaches and no bad dreams.

I was probably a different kind of cat for the counselors and psychologists in the treatment centers. The bulk of the counseling indicates that you are a "recovering" or "overcoming" addict. They would say once an addict, always an addict. I had to reject that notion for me. I had to accept that God set me free and so I was free. I am a former addict. I am now redeemed, forgiven and delivered. I actively participate in my deliverance. That means I stay in the word of God, I minister to those I used to get high with in safe boundaries, I profess what I used to be and then glorify God for what I am.

I am not an addict and of course there are some who will read that and have a problem with it. I cannot argue the point; I can only say that it is what I speak over my life. I am not an addict. I do have some bad memories from the things that I have done; but God continues to heal me from even those things.

I went through those extended seasons of not being able to make an intelligent decision, because I was constantly high. You learn to smooth out a high so that you are able to function in a more normal sense. I knew better than any counselor how my life had gotten so out of control because my high days started outweighing my bad days. So when I poured out the darkest crevices of my soul in group and individual counseling; I decided that was it for me. I had begun to learn so much about God during that time and I was learning that everything I was reading and absorbing of Him was proving itself true and powerful in my life.

God took the taste of cocaine out of my mouth and the desire for its deceptive emotions out of my heart. Treatment centers helped but they could not do it. Doctors helped, but they could not do it. Only when I applied the word of God did deliverance abide with me. I believe it emphatically. I remember crying out to this God, the one my mom introduced me to when she would take her kids to Sunday school. I knew of God, but it was an intimate and applicable relationship with Him that saved my life and sent the demon back to hell.

CHAPTER 12

REMEMEBER THAT DRUGS ARE A DEMON

In the course of writing this book, a tragedy involving drugs rang out on the evening news in Daytona. A young man beat his father to death because he had refused to give him money to buy drugs. In a drug-induced rage, he beat and stabbed his own father to death. If I could talk to him, I would tell him to try Christ. The demon he is fighting has escalated his use of him and he can not beat him by himself. Only a demonic spirit could cause a son to take his father's life like that.

We have to remember that drugs are a demon. They are a demon that feed off of so many things. There is misguided love, loss of love, rejection, self esteem, and rape/incest or molestation. Emotional traumas like feeling ignored or misunderstood, unheard can lead to drug use. So now I listen to my grandchildren differently. I try to listen to hear if there is any pain or lack in what they are saying and I talk to them up front about what I hear or what I feel they are expressing.

I do not and will not judge anyone's path away from drugs. I will instead pull them out as much as I can. I will offer them the same deliverer that went into the gates of hell for me. I will tell them that I know that I am done with it and they can be too. I am delivered.

1 John 2:12-14

[12] I write unto you, little children, because your sins are forgiven you for his name's sake.

[13] I write unto you, fathers, because ye have known him that is from the beginning. I write unto you, young men, because ye have overcome the wicked one. I write unto you, little children, because ye have known the Father.

¹⁴I have written unto you, fathers, because ye have known him that is from the beginning. I have written unto you, young men, because ye are strong, and the word of God abideth in you, and ye have overcome the wicked one.

Ephesians 5:8-20

⁸For ye were sometimes darkness, but now are ye light in the Lord: walk as children of light:

⁹(For the fruit of the Spirit is in all goodness and righteousness and truth);

¹⁰Proving what is acceptable unto the Lord.

¹¹And have no fellowship with the unfruitful works of darkness, but rather reprove them.

¹²For it is a shame even to speak of those things which are done of them in secret.

¹³But all things that are reproved are made manifest by the light: for whatsoever doth make manifest is light.

¹⁴Wherefore he saith, Awake thou that sleepest, and arise from the dead, and Christ shall give thee light.

¹⁵See then that ye walk circumspectly, not as fools, but as wise,

¹⁶Redeeming the time, because the days are evil.

¹⁷Wherefore be ye not unwise, but understanding what the will of the Lord is.

¹⁸And be not drunk with wine, wherein is excess; but be filled with the Spirit;

¹⁹Speaking to yourselves in psalms and hymns and spiritual songs, singing and making melody in your heart to the Lord;

²⁰Giving thanks always for all things unto God and the Father in the name of our Lord Jesus Christ;

This passage of scripture speaks to my spirit. It is God's reminder to me to turn from every spirit that causes me to act outside of His will. I can not be drunk with wine or high with cocaine, or any other narcotic and be filled with His Spirit. I have been filled with all of the above and I can say unequivocally that being filled with the spirit is so much better.

While I lived with crack, the streets (and some that I called friends), plastered me with many labels. They called me a slut. They said I was no good. They scandalized me and waited with great anticipation for my demise. Interestingly, there are many who see me stand by the sacred desk and preach God's word that can not get past those labels. They see me and many whisper from the pews, "that was the one that was strung out."

There are people who I was on drugs with and they see me and say, "Wow if Jesus can change you He can change me." I tell them yes he definitely can. That is what it is all about. I still have challenges – and no – they do not include crack cocaine. It is like David and Goliath, God is teaching me to take the head off of my giants – because the head cuts off the circulation of life.

One of my giants has always been rejection. I had to take its head off especially with the ministry my sister and I were called into. I could not worry about rejection if I was going to offer salvation and deliverance to those still struggling with crack. So I take my ears off of the remarks about how I used to be where they are, or how do I know I won't be back – instead I focus on my purpose; to bring you to this new life. This new life I live brings with it a high whose side effects are promises, provision, prosperity and everlasting life. I stand victoriously in the confidence of God.

When I began my journey into the fullness of Christ, there were ministers, pastors and deacons that tried to minister to me. That ministry however was of little to no effect, because you see while they spoke you need to leave drugs alone, they were yet getting high. My testimony had to be sincere and complete. I could not judge them but I could not allow them to offer me a false deliverance either.

You have to participate in your deliverance. You may not need deliverance from drugs like I did. You may struggle with pornography or another sexual sin. Perhaps you struggle with being unable to handle your finances – what ever your demon is you can be delivered from it and you must participate in that deliverance. That means face your giants, separate from the unclean things whether they are: friends, family, places or associations. Be strong in Christ and allow Him to be strong in you. I am blessed to have gone from a mess to a miracle to a messenger and this is my message – He who the son sets free is free indeed, accept His freedom.

2 Corinthians 5:17

[17]Therefore if any man be in Christ, he is a new creature: old things are passed away; behold, all things are become new.

An Afterword in Honor of Cyteria Freeman

I have been a therapist and counselor for most of my life, and taught at the undergraduate level over the last twenty years. It is one of my greatest honors to be asked by Ms. Freeman to write this afterword; but, the honor is really in celebration of her life and her recovery from addiction and the things that haunted her past. Many of these things should never have to happen to anyone, even if they do have an addiction. The fact that she has changed so tremendously is a celebration of life and the gospel.

The inspiration that I hope you will feel from her story, provided to our college, our community and everyone who reads or hears about this book, is shown by the changes I have seen in her in the academic setting. Since 2006, when she started taking classes in the Human Services Program, until today, the change in her life—her Delivery—is a transformation to hold up to others as a role model and an example of faith.

The Human Services Program deals with counseling, losing others, addictions, emotional and psychological problems and traumas. It is not an easy Program—psychologically nor academically. I did not know if she would make it. She was committed to working and we, quite frankly did not have enough evening classes for her to complete the Program. I did not see her often and then she did not come back one semester—Fall of 2007. I thought to myself, sometimes you just have to let them go.

And then suddenly, she reappeared late in the Fall term of 2008; she wanted to re--enter the Program. In Human Services, we know all about giving people second chances, more if need be. Some of us also know it is not about us but about our Higher Power, our Lord and Savior. From the time she started school in January 2009 until today, she has achieved academically and in her service to the community. She offers support to others: Students, faculty and staff.

I am deeply grateful to her for her words of wisdom and her actions in class. She has portrayed herself as Delivered rather than having overcome her past. However, I see someone who was transformed. She is quiet when necessary and speaks out when necessary. Her academic career was good, but inhibited by her writing skills. She obtained a writing coach. Her past had interfered emotionally in the work needed for a person to work in Human Services. That requires emotional and psychological strength as I said. But now, her work has been outstanding, and she is providing the message of emotional and psychological support: An inspiration to others in class and the college. It took emotional and psychological strength to become what she is and what she offers to others. You simply cannot, I believe, offer what is necessary to others unless you have been able to let go of the past—that transformation occurred, she says, as she was Delivered. I hope that she accepts, and all of you who are reading this accept, at least in part, my belief that she had to be willing, humble, and courageous in order to take the steps necessary to become a messenger. She became strong through her weaknesses and psychologically healthy.

She is not just a college student but a minister of the gospel. She speaks what she believes, has put gossip and anger behind her so that her beautiful person inside could come out to be an inspiration and give others the courage to take the steps that she did in order to be Delivered. I want to congratulate her and hope that she is able to provide the ministry to lift you up as she has lifted me; that she is able to show the light on the path for others to recover or avoid the pitfalls she fell into. I hope her ministry is able to be a rainbow that can shed light on the path so that others do not choose to use drugs or fall into any of the other things that are in the world to entrap us. And if they do so choose, I hope her message can help give them the courage to step forth and be delivered from the pain and the shame and all of the other emotional and psychological traps that are part of the baggage.

Blessings,
Dr. Patti Hall-Pennell

A Prayer of Deliverance

Heavenly Father, the Most High God, the God of deliverance. I come to you in great faith and in the name of your son Jesus the Christ, asking if you would grant deliverance to everyone who prays this prayer. I stand upon your Word because your Word is a lamp unto my feet and a light unto my path. Psalms 119: 105 in your Word declares, where the Spirit of the Lord is there is freedom. Second Corinthians 3:17 says and help me not to be entangled again with the yoke of bondage. And is it is written in your Word in Galatians 5:1, in Jesus name, I bind and take authority over all kinds of addictions – sex, alcohol, crack, cocaine, marijuana and all pharmaceuticals! I loose power, strength and deliverance because whom the Son makes free is free indeed.

In Jesus name, I pray – Amen.

The Pecan Tree Publishing Collection

www.pecantreebooks.com

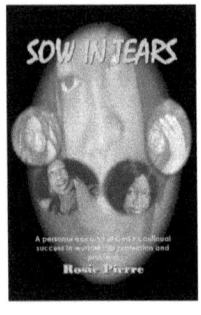

The Digital Publications of Pecan Tree Publishing

www.ingramcontent.com/pod-product-compliance
Lightning Source LLC
Chambersburg PA
CBHW071157090426
42736CB00012B/2361